A 31-day Prayer Venture

for every believer

Dennis Gorton

adapted from Andrew Murray

Christian Publications
3825 Hartzdale Drive, Camp Hill, PA 17011

Faithful, biblical publishing since 1883

ISBN: 0-87509-543-7

Printed in the United States of America

94 95 96 97 98 5 4 3 2 1

INTRODUCTION

First Thessalonians 5:17 says, "pray continually." Most of us are more familiar with this quote from the King James Version, "pray without ceasing." Who can do this? How can one do it who is surrounded by cares of daily life? How can a mother love her child without ceasing? How can the eyelid without ceasing hold itself ready to protect the eye? How can I breathe, feel and hear without ceasing? If the spiritual life is healthy, under the fullness of the Holy Spirit, praying without ceasing will be natural.

But what does it mean to pray without ceasing? Does it refer to continual acts of prayer or to the spirit of prayerfulness? It includes both. Christ's example shows us this. We have to get away for special seasons of prayer and we are at times to stay there in continuing prayer. We must also walk in God's presence with our whole heart set upon heavenly things. Without set times of prayer the spirit of prayer will be dull and without continual prayerfulness these set times become rote.

Does "pray without ceasing" refer to prayer for ourselves or for others? Both! It is because many confine it to themselves that they fail in practicing it. It is only when the branch gives itself to bear fruit, more fruit, much fruit, that it can live a healthy life and expect a rich inflow of Spirit life for growth. This is true not only for the individual but also for the corporate body in its prayer life.

So the next logical question is, how can I learn to pray? The best way of learning to do a thing is to do it. Begin by setting apart some time every day, say 10 or 15 minutes, in which you say to God and to yourself that you are coming to Him as an intercessor for others. Jesus has appointed and chosen you to pray for yourself and others. If you do not feel any special urgency, at first, do not let that hinder you. Quietly tell the Lord Jesus about your lack; believe that the Holy Spirit is in you to teach you to pray, and be assured that if you begin, God will help you. He cannot help you, however, unless you begin and keep on.

Where do I start? Most of us have plenty to pray for if we give it a few moments of thought, but to give us some guidelines the following material is laid out in a format of a prayer guide for 31 days. It is meant to be used month by month, until we know more fully how to follow the Spirit's leading in prayer. If you will give this 31-day venture into prayer just three months, I believe you will see your life changed and your church begin to respond in spiritual growth, which in its proper context always produces numerical growth.

A 31-DAY PRAYER VENTURE

You will notice for every day two headings: "What to Pray" and "How to Pray." The hints under how to pray are meant to remind us of the spiritual nature of prayer, of the need for divine help and to encourage faith in the certainty that God, through the Spirit, will give us grace to pray correctly. It is difficult to take your place boldly and to dare to believe that you will be heard; therefore, take a few moments each day to listen to God's voice reminding you of how certainly even you will be heard, and calling you on to pray in faith.

Scripture calls us to pray for many things. The church is now so much larger than when the New Testament was written, the kinds of ministry so much more diverse, the needs of the church and the world are so much better known, that we need to take time and thought to see where prayer is really needed. An attempt has been made in this guide to indicate what the major subjects are that need prayer. You will need to fill in the specifics from your life and ministry.

DAY 1

What to Pray: For the Power of the Holy Spirit

I pray that out of his glorious riches he may strengthen you with power through his Spirit in your inner being . . . (Ephesians 3:16)

"Wait for the gift my Father promised . . ." (Acts 1:4)

Pray for the fuller manifestation of the grace and power of the Spirit of God in the removal of all that is contrary to His will, so that we do not grieve the Holy Spirit, but that He may work in greater power in the church for the exaltation of Jesus Christ our Lord.

God has one promise to and through His exalted Son; our Lord has one gift to His Church; the Church has one need; all prayer unites in the one petition: the power of the Holy Spirit. Make it your one prayer.

How to Pray: As a Child Asks a Father

"Which of you fathers, if your son asks for a fish, will give him a snake instead? . . . If you then, though you are evil, know how to give good gifts to your children, how much more will your Father in heaven give the Holy Spirit to those who ask him!" (Luke 11:11, 13)

Ask as simply and trustfully as a child asks for a cookie. You can do this because "you are sons, God sent the Spirit of his Son into our hearts, the Spirit who calls out, '*Abba*, Father' " (Galatians 4:6). The Spirit is in you to give you childlike confidence. In faith knowing He is praying in you, ask for the power of the Holy Spirit to be manifest in your life, your church, the workplace, the hospital or anywhere else you will be dealing with people.

Specific Needs

___

___

DAY 2

What to Pray: For the Spirit of Supplication

The Spirit himself intercedes for us . . . (Romans 8:26)
"And I will pour out . . . a spirit of . . . supplication." (Zechariah 12:10)

Worldwide evangelization depends first of all upon a revival of prayer. Deep down at the bottom of our spiritless life is the need for the forgotten secret of prevailing, worldwide prayer.

Every child of God has the Holy Spirit in him to pray. God waits to give the Spirit in full measure. Ask for yourself, and all who join you, the outpouring of the spirit of supplication. Pray for the missionaries you know personally and those who spoke in your last missions conference.

How to Pray: In the Spirit

And pray in the Spirit on all occasions with all kinds of prayers and requests. (Ephesians 6:18)
Pray in the Holy Spirit. (Jude 20)

Our Lord gave His disciples on resurrection day the Holy Spirit to enable them to wait for the full outpouring on the day of Pentecost. It is only in the power of the Spirit already in us, acknowledged and yielded to, that we can pray for His fuller manifestation. Ask God to fill you and use you in His way.

Specific Needs

____

____

____

____

____

DAY 3

What to Pray: For All the Saints

And pray in the Spirit on all occasions with all kinds of prayers and requests. With this in mind, be alert and always keep on praying for all the saints. (Ephesians 6:18)

Every member of a body is interested in the welfare of the whole and exists to help and complete the others. Believers are one body and ought to pray for all the saints. Pray for those in your local church, then your community and even district. This unselfish expression of love is the proof that Christ's Spirit is teaching us to pray. Pray first for those you know best and then for the believers around you.

How to Pray: In the Love of the Spirit

"By this all men will know that you are my disciples, if you love one another." (John 13:35)
"That all of them may be one, Father, just as you are in me and I am in you." (John 17:21)
I urge you, brothers, by our Lord Jesus Christ and by the love of the Spirit, to join me in my struggle by praying to God for me. (Romans 15:30)
Above all, love each other deeply, because love covers over a multitude of sins. (1 Peter 4:8)

If we are to pray we must love. Let us say to God we do love all His saints; let us especially say that we love those we know well. Let us pray with fervent love, in the love of the Spirit, for those whom we may have a hard time relating to in the church.

Specific Needs

____

____

DAY 4

What to Pray: For the Spirit of Holiness

It is God's will that you should be sanctified . . .
(1 Thessalonians 4:3)
But just as he who called you is holy, so be holy in all you do; for it is written: "Be holy, because I am holy." (1 Peter 1:15-16)

Pray for individuals in the church, that the spirit of holiness may rule. Pray for new converts, for the believers in your own neighborhood or congregation, for any you know have special need here. Think of their special need, weakness or sin, and pray that God will make them holy. Pray for yourself.

How to Pray: Trusting in God's Omnipotence

Trust in the LORD with all your heart and lean not on your own understanding; in all your ways acknowledge him, and he will make your paths straight. (Proverbs 3:5-6)

The things that are impossible with men are possible with God. When we think of the great things we ask for and how little we can do to make them happen, we must trust. Prayer is not only wishing or asking, but believing and accepting. Be still before God and ask Him to allow you to know Him as the Almighty One, and leave your prayers with Him who does wonders.

Specific Needs

____

____

____

____

____

DAY 5

What to Pray: That God's People May Be Kept from the World

"Holy Father, protect them by the power of your name—the name you gave me—so that they may be one as we are one. . . . My prayer is not that you take them out of the world but that you protect them from the evil one. They are not of the world, even as I am not of it." (John 17:11, 15-16)

On the last night Jesus asked three things for His disciples: that they might be "kept" as those who are not of the world; that they might be sanctified; that they might be one in love. You cannot do better then pray as Jesus prayed. Ask that God's people may be kept separate from the world and its spirit; that they, by the Holy Spirit, may live as those who are not of the world while serving in the world.

How to Pray: Having Confidence before God

Dear friends, if our hearts do not condemn us, we have confidence before God and receive from him anything we ask, because we obey his commands and do what pleases him. (1 John 3:21-22)

Learn these words by heart. Get them into your mind and being. Join the ranks of those who, with John, draw near to God with a confident heart that does not condemn them. In this spirit pray for your brother who sins (1 John 5:16). In the quiet confidence of an obedient child plead for those of your church who may be giving way to sin.

Specific Needs

____

____

____

DAY 6

What to Pray: For the Spirit of Love in the Church

"May they be brought to complete unity to let the world know that you sent me and have loved them even as you have loved me." (John 17:23)
But the fruit of the Spirit is love. (Galatians 5:22)

Believers are one in Christ, as He is one with the Father. The love of God rests on them and can dwell in them. Pray that the power of the Holy Spirit may so work His love in believers that the world may see and know God's love in them. Pray much for this.

How to Pray: As One of God's "Callers"

I have posted watchmen on your walls, O Jerusalem; they will never be silent day or night. You who call on the LORD, give yourselves no rest. (Isaiah 62:6)

Study these words until your whole soul is filled with the consciousness: I am appointed to call on the Lord. Enter God's presence in that faith. Study the world's need with this thought—it is my work to intercede; the Holy Spirit will teach me for what and how. Let it be an abiding consciousness. My great life work, like Christ's, is intercession—to pray for believers and those who do not yet know God.

Specific Needs

____

____

____

____

____

DAY 7

What to Pray: For the Power of the Holy Spirit on Pastors

I urge you, brothers, by our Lord Jesus Christ and by the love of the Spirit, to join me in my struggle by praying to God for me. (Romans 15:30)

As you help us by your prayers. (2 Corinthians 1:11)

Think of the great multitude of pastors there are in Christ's church. They have great need of prayer. What a power they might be if they were all clothed with the power of the Holy Spirit! Pray definitely for this. Think of your own pastor and ask it very specifically for him. Connect every thought of the ministry, in your town or neighborhood or the world, with the prayer that all may be filled with the Spirit. Plead for them the promise "stay in the city until you have been clothed with power from on high" (Luke 24:49) and "you will receive power when the Holy Spirit comes on you" (Acts 1:8).

How to Pray: In Secret

"But when you pray, go into your room, close the door and pray to your Father, who is unseen. Then your Father, who sees what is done in secret, will reward you." (Matthew 6:6)

He went up on a mountainside by himself to pray. (Matthew 14:23)

Jesus . . . withdrew again to a mountain by himself. (John 6:15)

Stop and think as you are alone with God: here I am now, face to face with God, to intercede for His servants. Do not think you have no influence, or that your prayer will not be missed. Your prayer and faith will make a difference. Cry in secret to God for His chosen church leaders.

Specific Needs

DAY 8

What to Pray: For Lost People in Your Neighborhood

"But you will receive power when the Holy Spirit comes on you; and you will be my witnesses in Jerusalem, . . ." (Acts 1:8)

The disciples were witnesses first in their home areas. Our friends, relatives and neighbors are people who will spend an eternity in hell separated from God. "All have sinned"; no one is righteous! Pray that God will so arrange people's lives that they will be more receptive to your witness of what God is doing in your life. Pray for their conversion and be prepared to live and share Jesus with them.

How to Pray: With Definite Petitions

"What do you want me to do for you?" (Luke 18:41)

The Lord knew what the man wanted, and yet He asked him. Speaking our wish gives focus to the transaction in which we are engaged with God, and thus awakens faith and expectation. Be very definite in your petitions. Just think of the lost around you, and ask and expect God to make them open to the gospel in answer to the prayers of His people. Then ask still more definitely for opportunities to share with those around you. Intercession is not the breathing out of pious wishes; its aim is, in believing, persevering prayer, to see men and women saved.

Specific Needs

____

____

____

____

DAY 9

What to Pray: For God's Spirit on Our Missionary Work

While they were worshiping the Lord and fasting, the Holy Spirit said, "Set apart for me Barnabas and Saul for the work to which I have called them." (Acts 13:2)

The evangelization of the world depends first of all upon a revival of prayer. Deeper than the need for men and women is the need for the secret of prevailing, worldwide prayer.

Pray that our missionary work may be done in this spirit—waiting on God, hearing the voice of the Spirit, sending forth men with fasting and prayer. Pray that in our churches, our missionary interest and missionary work may be in the power of the Holy Spirit and of prayer. It is the Spirit-filled, praying church that will send out Spirit-filled missionaries.

How to Pray: Take Time

I am a man of prayer. (Psalm 109:4)
"And will give our attention to prayer and the ministry of the word." (Acts 6:4)
Jesus . . . spent the night praying to God. (Luke 6:12)
Do not be quick with your mouth, do not be hasty in your heart to utter anything before God. (Ecclesiastes 5:2)

Time is a major standard of value. The time we give is a proof of the interest we have. We need time with God to realize His presence, to wait for Him to make Himself known, to consider the needs we plead for, to take our place in Christ, to pray until we can believe that we have received. Take time in prayer, and pray down blessing on the missionary work of the church.

Specific Needs

DAY 10

What to Pray: For God's Spirit on Our Missionaries

"But you will receive power when the Holy Spirit comes on you; and you will be my witnesses in Jerusalem, and in all Judea and Samaria, and to the ends of the earth." (Acts 1:8)

What the world needs today is not only more missionaries but the outpouring of God's Spirit on everyone whom He has sent out to work for Him in the foreign field.

God always gives His servants power equal to the work He asks of them. Think of the difficulty of this work, casting Satan out of his strongholds. Pray that everyone who takes part in it may receive and do His work in the power of the Holy Spirit. Think of the difficulties of our missionaries, and pray for them.

How to Pray: Trusting God's Faithfulness

For he who promised is faithful. (Hebrews 10:23)

Think of God's promises to His Son concerning His kingdom; to the church, concerning the lost; to His servants, concerning their work; to yourself, concerning your prayer; and pray in assurance that He is faithful. He only waits for prayer and faith to fulfill them. "The one who calls you" (to pray) "is faithful and he will do it" (1 Thessalonians 5:24).

Take up individual missionaries, make yourself one with them, and pray until you know that you are heard. Begin to live for Christ's kingdom as the one thing worth living for!

Specific Needs

____

____

____

DAY 11

What to Pray: For More Laborers

"Ask the Lord of the harvest, therefore, to send out workers into his harvest field." (Matthew 9:38)

What a remarkable call of the Lord Jesus for help! What an honor put upon prayer! What a proof that God desires prayer and will hear it!

Pray for laborers, for our students in seminary and Bible college, that they will know His call. Pray that our churches may teach their youth to seek for the sending of the Holy Spirit, that all believers may hold themselves ready to be sent, or to pray for those who can go.

How to Pray: In Faith, Doubting Nothing

"Have faith in God," Jesus answered. "I tell you the truth, if anyone says to this mountain, 'Go, throw yourself into the sea,' and does not doubt in his heart but believes that what he says will happen, it will be done for him." (Mark 11:22-23)

Have faith in God! Ask Him to make Himself known to you as the faithful, mighty God, who works all in all. You will be encouraged to believe that He can provide suitable and sufficient laborers, however impossible this appears. Apply this to every opening where a good worker is needed. The work is God's. He can give the right worker. But He must be asked.

Specific Needs

____

____

____

____

____

DAY 12

What to Pray: For the Spirit to Convince the World of Sin

"I will send him to you. When he comes, he will convict the world of guilt in regard to sin . . ." (John 16:7-8)

God's one desire, the one object of Christ's being manifest, is to take away sin. The first work of the Spirit in the world is conviction of sin. Without this there is no deep or abiding revival, no powerful conversion. Pray that the gospel may be proclaimed in such power that men may see that they have rejected and crucified Christ and cry out, "What shall we do?" Pray earnestly for a mighty power of conviction of sin wherever the gospel is proclaimed.

How to Pray: Stir Up Yourself to Take Hold of God's Strength

But Jacob replied, "I will not let you go unless you bless me." (Genesis 32:26)

No one calls on your name or strives to lay hold of you. (Isaiah 64:7)

Fan into flame the gift of God, which is in you . . . (2 Timothy 1:6)

First, take hold of God's strength. God is a Spirit. I cannot take hold of Him, and hold Him fast, but by the Spirit. Take hold of God's strength and hold on till it has done for you what He has promised. Pray for the power of the Spirit to convict of sin. Give your whole heart and will to it, and say, "I will not let You go unless You bless me."

Specific Needs

____

____

DAY 13

What to Pray: For the Spirit of Fire

Those who are left in Zion, who remain in Jerusalem, will be called holy, all who are recorded among the living in Jerusalem. The Lord will wash away the filth of the women of Zion; he will cleanse the bloodstains from Jerusalem by a spirit of judgment and a spirit of fire. (Isaiah 4:3-4)

A washing by fire! A cleansing by judgment! He who has passed through this shall be called holy. The power of blessing for the world depends upon the spiritual state of the Church. Judgment must begin at the house of God. There must be conviction of sin. Beseech God to give His Spirit as a spirit of judgment and a spirit of fire to discover and burn out sin in His people.

How to Pray: In the Name of Christ

"And I will do whatever you ask in my name, so that the Son may bring glory to the Father. You may ask me for anything in my name, and I will do it." (John 14:13-14)

Ask in the name of your Redeemer who sits upon the throne. Ask what He has promised, what He gave His blood for, that sin may be put away from among His people. Ask for the spirit of deep conviction of sin to come upon His people. Ask for the spirit of fire. Ask in His name and look for the answer. Pray that the Church may be blessed and be made a blessing in the world.

Specific Needs

____

____

____

____

DAY 14

What to Pray: For the Church of the Future

They would not be like their forefathers—a stubborn and rebellious generation, whose hearts were not loyal to God, whose spirits were not faithful to him. (Psalm 78:8)
"I will pour out my Spirit on your offspring, and my blessing on your descendants." (Isaiah 44:3)

Pray for the upcoming generation. Think of the young men, young women and children of your church and pray for all the persons who work with them. Pray that they may honor Christ and that the Holy Spirit will fill them. Pray for the youth of your own neighborhood.

How to Pray: With the Whole Heart

May he give you the desire of your heart and make all your plans succeed. (Psalm 20:4)
You have granted him the desire of his heart. (Psalm 21:2)
I call with all my heart; answer me, O LORD. (Psalm 119:145)

God listens to every prayer with His whole heart. Each time we pray the infinite God is there to hear. He asks that in each prayer the whole person shall be there, and that we pray with our whole heart. Christ gave Himself to God for men and so He takes up every need. If once we seek God with our whole heart, the whole heart will be in every prayer with which we come to God. Pray with your whole heart for the youth.

Specific Needs

____

____

____

DAY 15

What to Pray: For Schools and Colleges

"As for me, this is my covenant with them," says the LORD. "My Spirit, who is on you, and my words that I have put in your mouth will not depart from your mouth, or from the mouths of your children, or from the mouths of their descendants from this time on and forever," says the LORD. (Isaiah 59:21)

The future of the Church and the world depends, to a greater extent than we conceive, on education. The Church may be seeking to evangelize the lost and at the same time be giving up her own children to secular and materialistic influences. Pray for schools and colleges. Pray for all godly teachers.

How to Pray: Not Limiting God

Again and again they put God to the test; they vexed the Holy One of Israel. (Psalm 78:41)
And he did not do many miracles there because of their lack of faith. (Matthew 13:58)
"Is anything too hard for the LORD?" (Genesis 18:14)
"Ah, Sovereign LORD, you have made the heavens and the earth by your great power and outstretched arm. Nothing is too hard for you.
"I am the LORD, the God of all mankind. Is anything too hard for me?" (Jeremiah 32:17, 27)

Beware of limiting God, not only by unbelief, but by thinking that you know what He can do. Expect unexpected things, "immeasurably more than all we ask or imagine" (Ephesians 3:20). Each time you intercede, be quiet first and worship God in His glory. Think of what He can do, of how He delights to hear Jesus, of your place in Jesus, and expect great things.

Specific Needs

DAY 16

What to Pray: For the Power of the Holy Spirit in Our Sunday Schools

But this is what the LORD says: "Yes, captives will be taken from warriors, and plunder retrieved from the fierce; I will contend with those who contend with you, and your children I will save." (Isaiah 49:25)

Every part of the work of God's Church is His work. He must do it. Prayer is the confession that He will. It is the surrender of ourselves into His hands to let Him work in us and through us. Pray for the thousands of Sunday school teachers that they may be filled with His Spirit. Pray for your own Sunday school. Pray for the spiritual growth of children, youth and adults.

How to Pray: Boldly

We have a great high priest . . . Jesus the Son of God. . . . Let us then approach the throne of grace with confidence. (Hebrews 4:14, 16)

These hints to help us in our work of intercession, what are they doing for us? Making us conscious of our feebleness in prayer? Thank God for this. It is the very first lesson we need on the way to pray "the effectual fervent prayer . . . [that] availeth much" (James 5:16, KJV). Let us continue taking each subject boldly to the throne of grace. As we pray we will learn to pray, to believe and to expect with increasing boldness.

Specific Needs

___

___

___

DAY 17

What to Pray: For Those in Authority

I urge, then, first of all, that requests, prayers, intercession and thanksgiving be made for everyone—for kings and all those in authority, that we may live peaceful and quiet lives in all godliness and holiness. (1 Timothy 2:1-2)

What faith in the power of prayer! A few weak and unknown Christians can influence the governments of the world and help in securing peace and quietness. Let us believe that prayer releases the power of God in His rule of the world. Let us pray for our country and its authorities; for all the governments of the world; for leaders in cities or districts in which we are interested. When God's people unite in this, they may count upon their prayers' effect. Let faith be exercised.

How to Pray: The Prayer before God as Incense

Another angel, who had a golden censer, came and stood at the altar. He was given much incense to offer, with the prayers of all the saints, on the golden altar before the throne. The smoke of the incense, together with the prayers of the saints, went up before God from the angel's hand. Then the angel took the censer, filled it with fire from the altar, and hurled it on the earth; and there came peals of thunder, rumblings, flashes of lightning and an earthquake. (Revelation 8:3-5)

The same censer brings the prayer of the saints before God and casts fire upon the earth. The prayers that go up to heaven have their share in the history of this earth. Be sure that your prayers enter God's presence.

Specific Needs

____

____

DAY 18

What to Pray: For Peace

I urge, then, first of all, that requests, prayers, intercession and thanksgiving be made for everyone—for kings and all those in authority, that we may live peaceful and quiet lives in all godliness and holiness. This is good, and pleases God our Savior. (1 Timothy 2:1-3)

He makes wars cease to the ends of the earth. (Psalm 46:9)

God can, in answer to the prayer of His people, give peace. Let us pray for it and for the rule of righteousness on which peace can be established. Only God's peace is eternal. Only God's peace brings true peace on earth.

How to Pray: With My Mind and Spirit

So what shall I do? I will pray with my spirit, but I will also pray with my mind. (1 Corinthians 14:15)

We need to pray with our spirits if we are to take hold of God in faith and power. We need to pray with our minds if we are really to enter deeply into the needs we bring before Him. Take time to think through each subject; the nature, the extent, the urgency of the request. Remember God's promises as revealed in His Word. Let the mind affect the heart. Pray with your mind and with your spirit.

Specific Needs

____

____

____

____

____

DAY 19

What to Pray: For the Power of the Holy Spirit

Having a form of godliness but denying its power. (2 Timothy 3:5)

"You have a reputation of being alive, but you are dead." (Revelation 3:1)

There are multitudes of nominal Christians. The state of the majority is unspeakable. Formality, worldliness, ungodliness, rejection of Christ's service, ignorance and indifference prevail to a large extent. We pray for the lost . . . so let us pray for those bearing Christ's name.

Sometimes one feels as if he ought to give up his life and cry day and night to God for them. Remember to pray for God's power through the Spirit to work.

How to Pray: In Deep Stillness of Soul

My soul finds rest in God alone; my salvation comes from him. (Psalm 62:1)

Prayer has its power in God alone. The nearer a man comes to God, the deeper he enters into God's will; the more he takes hold of God, the more power he can expect in prayer.

God must reveal Himself. If it pleases Him to make Himself known, He can make the heart conscious of His presence. Our posture must be that of holy reverence, quiet waiting and adoration.

As your month of intercession moves on and you feel the greatness of your work, be still before God. Thus you will receive power to pray.

Specific Needs

____

____

DAY 20

What to Pray: For God's Spirit on the Lost

See, they will come from afar—some from the north, some from the west, some from the region of Aswan. (Isaiah 49:12)
Envoys will come from Egypt; Cush will submit herself to God. (Psalm 68:31)

Pray for the lost who are yet without the Word. Every land from China to the Philippines to Africa is populated with multitudes who have yet to know our Christ. If Christ gave His life for them, how can we do less? You can give yourself up to intercede for them. The minutes you give will make you feel this is not enough. God's Spirit will draw you on. Ask God to give you some country to pray for. Can anything be nobler than to do as Christ did? Give your life for the lost of the world.

How to Pray: With Confident Expectation of an Answer

Call to me and I will answer you and tell you great and unsearchable things you do not know. (Jeremiah 33:3)
"This is what the Sovereign LORD says: 'Once again I will yield to the plea of the house of Israel and do this for them . . .' " (Ezekiel 36:37)

Both texts refer to promises made, but their fulfillment depends upon prayer. Pray for God's fulfillment of His promises to His Son and His Church. Expect the answer. Plead for the lost. Pray God's promises.

Specific Needs

DAY 21

What to Pray: For God's Spirit on Ethnic Minorities

Brothers, my heart's desire and prayer to God for the Israelites is that they may be saved. (Romans 10:1)

The author of Romans prayed specifically for the Jews, an ethnic minority in Roman culture. Today America is being flooded with people from every nation. Displaced and lonely, they are open to the message of the gospel. Pray for their salvation.

How to Pray: With the Intercession of the Holy Spirit

We do not know what we ought to pray for, but the Spirit himself intercedes for us with groans that words cannot express. (Romans 8:26)

In your ignorance and weakness believe in the secret indwelling and intercession of the Holy Spirit within you. Yield yourself to His life and leading habitually. He will help your infirmities in prayer. Plead the promises of God even where you do not see how they are to be fulfilled. God knows the mind of the Spirit, because He makes intercession for His people according to the will of God. Pray with the simplicity of a little child; pray with the holy awe and reverence of one in whom God's Spirit dwells.

Specific Needs

____

____

____

____

DAY 22

What to Pray: For All Who Are Suffering

Remember those in prison as if you were their fellow prisoners, and those who are mistreated as if you yourselves were suffering. (Hebrews 13:3)

What a world of suffering we live in! How Jesus sacrificed all and identified Himself with it! What suffering there is around those who know God and who know Him not. In our own neighborhood, how many need help or comfort? Let us have a heart for and let us think of the suffering. It will stir us to pray, to work, to hope, to love more. And in a way and time we know not, God will hear our prayer.

How to Pray: Praying Always, and Not Giving Up

Then Jesus told his disciples a parable to show them that they should always pray and not give up. (Luke 18:1)

Have you begun to believe that prayer is the help for this sinful world and what a need there is of unceasing prayer? The very greatness of the task makes us despair. What can our few minutes of intercession do? It is right that we should feel this! This is the way in which God is calling and preparing us to give our lives to prayer. Give yourself totally to God for people, and amid all your work your heart will be drawn out to people in love, and drawn up to God in dependence and expectation. To a heart so led by the Holy Spirit it is possible to pray always and not give up.

Specific Needs

____

____

____

____

DAY 23

What to Pray: For the Holy Spirit in Your Own Work

To this end I labor, struggling with all his energy, which so powerfully works in me. (Colossians 1:29)

You have your own special work; make it a work of intercession. Paul labored according to the working of God in him. Remember, God is not only the Creator, but the great Workman, who works all in all. You can only do your work in His strength, by Him working in you through the Spirit. Intercede for those among whom you work until God gives you life for them.

How to Pray: In God's Very Presence

Come near to God and he will come near to you. (James 4:8)

The nearness of God gives rest and power in prayer. "Come near to God." Seek nearness to Him and He will give it. "He will come near to you." Then it becomes easy to pray in faith.

Remember that when God takes you into a venture of intercession it is more for your own sake than for others. You have to be trained to love, to wait, to pray and to believe. Only persevere. Learn to set yourself in His presence, to wait quietly for the assurance that He comes near. Enter His holy presence, wait there and spread your work before Him. Intercede for the persons you are working with. Get a blessing from God, His Spirit in your own heart, for them.

Specific Needs

____

____

____

____

DAY 24

What to Pray: For the Spirit of Your Own Congregation

"Beginning at Jerusalem." (Luke 24:47)

Each one of us is connected with some congregation of believers, who are to us the part of Christ's body with which we come into most direct contact. They have a special claim on our intercession. Let it be a settled matter between God and you that you are to labor in prayer on their behalf. Pray for the pastor and all leaders of the church. Pray for believers according to their needs. Pray for conversions. Pray for the power of the Spirit to be manifest. Join with others in secret definite petitions. Let intercession be a definite work, carried on as systematically as preaching or Sunday school. Pray expecting an answer.

How to Pray: Continually

I have posted watchmen on your walls, O Jerusalem; they will never be silent day or night. (Isaiah 62:6)
"And will not God bring about justice for his chosen ones, who cry out to him day and night?" (Luke 18:7)
Night and day we pray most earnestly that we may see you again and supply what is lacking in your faith. (1 Thessalonians 3:10)
The widow who is really in need and left all alone puts her hope in God and continues night and day to pray and to ask God for help. (1 Timothy 5:5)

When the glory of God, the love of Christ and the needs of men are revealed to us, the fire of this unceasing intercession will begin to burn in us for those who are near.

Specific Needs

DAY 25

What to Pray: For More Conversions

Therefore he is able to save completely those who come to God through him, because he always lives to intercede for them. (Hebrews 7:25)

"And will give our attention to prayer and the ministry of the word." . . . So the word of God spread. The number of disciples in Jerusalem increased rapidly, and a large number of priests became obedient to the faith. (Acts 6:4, 7)

Christ's power to save, and save completely, depends on His unceasing intercession. The apostles withdrawing themselves from other work to give themselves continually to prayer was followed by conversion and church growth.

As we give ourselves to intercession we shall have more and mightier conversions. Let us plead for this. Christ is exalted to give repentance. The Church exists with the divine purpose and promise of having conversions. Let us not be ashamed to confess our sin and weakness and to cry out to God for more conversions. Plead for the salvation of sinners you know and love.

How to Pray: In Deep Humility

"Yes, Lord," she said, "but even the dogs eat the crumbs that fall from their masters' table."

Then Jesus answered, "Woman, you have great faith! Your request is granted." (Matthew 15:27-28)

We often feel unworthy and unable to pray aright. To accept this and to be content to come and be blessed in your unworthiness is true humility. Let not your littleness or your greatness hinder you for a moment.

Specific Needs

DAY 26

What to Pray: For the Holy Spirit on New Converts

When they arrived, they prayed for them that they might receive the Holy Spirit, because the Holy Spirit had not yet come upon any of them; they had simply been baptized into the name of the Lord Jesus. (Acts 8:15-16)
Set his seal of ownership on us, and put his Spirit in our hearts as a deposit, guaranteeing what is to come. (2 Corinthians 1:22)

How many new converts remain weak; how many fall into sin; how many just do not grow? If we pray for the Church, its growth and devotion to God's service, let us pray especially for new converts. How many stand alone surrounded by temptation; how many have no teaching on the Spirit in them, nor the power of God to establish them; how many in foreign lands are surrounded by Satan's power? If you pray for the power of the Spirit in the Church, pray especially that every new convert may know that he may claim and receive the fullness of the Spirit.

How to Pray: Without Ceasing

"As for me, far be it from me that I should sin against the LORD by failing to pray for you." (1 Samuel 12:23)

It is sin against the Lord to cease praying. When once we begin to see how absolutely indispensable intercession is, we shall feel that to cease intercession is grievous sin. Let us ask for grace to take up our places as priests with joy and to give our lives to bring down the blessing of heaven.

Specific Needs

____

____

DAY 27

What to Pray: That God's People May Realize Their Calling

"I will make you into a great nation and I will bless you; . . . all peoples on earth will be blessed through you." (Genesis 12:2-3)
May God be gracious to us and bless us and make his face shine upon us, that your ways may be known on earth, your salvation among all nations. (Psalm 67:1-2)

Abraham was only blessed that he might be a blessing to all the earth. Israel prayed for blessing, that God might be known among nations. Every believer is blessed that he may carry God's blessing to the world. Cry to God that His people may know that every believer is to live for the interests of God and His kingdom. If this truth were taught, believed and practiced, what a revolution it would bring to our work! What a host of willing intercessors we would have!

How to Pray: As One Who Has Been Blessed

Then Peter said, "Silver or gold I do not have, but what I have I give you." (Acts 3:6)
The Holy Spirit came on them as he had come on us at the beginning. . . . So if God gave them the same gift as he gave us, who believed in the Lord Jesus Christ, who was I to think that I could oppose God? (Acts 11:15, 17)

As you pray for this great blessing on God's people, the Holy Spirit taking entire possession of them for God's service, yield yourself to God and claim Him anew by faith. Let your thoughts of personal shortcomings make you even more urgent in prayer for others. As the blessing comes to them, you too will be helped. With every prayer for conversion or mission work, pray that God's people may know how totally they belong to Him.

Specific Needs

DAY 28

What to Pray: That All God's People May Know the Holy Spirit

"The Spirit of truth. The world cannot accept him, because it neither sees him nor knows him. But you know him, for he lives with you and will be in you." (John 14:17)
Do you not know that your body is a temple of the Holy Spirit? (1 Corinthians 6:19)

The Holy Spirit is the power of God for the salvation of men. He only works as He dwells in the Church. He is given to enable believers to live totally as God would have them live in the full experience and witness of Him who saves completely. Ask God that every one of His people may know the Holy Spirit, that they may know His fullness in everyday life.

How to Pray: Wrestling in Prayer

Epaphras, who is one of you and a servant of Christ Jesus, sends greetings. He is always wrestling in prayer for you, that you may stand firm in all the will of God, mature and fully assured. (Colossians 4:12)

The believer who is in full health, whose heart is filled with God's Spirit, often wrestles in prayer. For what? That his fellow believers may stand firm in all the will of God, mature and fully assured. That they may know what God wills for them, how He calls them to live and be led and walk by the Holy Spirit. Labor in prayer that all God's children may know the truth.

Specific Needs

____

____

____

DAY 29

What to Pray: For the Spirit of Intercession

"You did not choose me, but I chose you and appointed you to go and bear fruit—fruit that will last. Then the Father will give you whatever you ask in my name." (John 15:16)
"Until now you have not asked for anything in my name. . . . In that day you will ask in my name." (John 16:24, 26)

Has not our prayer venture taught us how little we have prayed in the name of Jesus? He promised His disciples that when the Holy Spirit comes upon you, you shall ask in My name. Let our intercession today be for all God's children, that Christ may teach us the power of the Holy Spirit in us, what it is to live in His fullness and to yield ourselves to His work within us. The Church and the world need nothing as much as a mighty spirit of intercession to bring down the power of God on earth. Pray for the descent from heaven of the spirit of intercession for a great prayer renewal.

How to Pray: Abiding in Christ

"If you remain in me and my words remain in you, ask whatever you wish, and it will be given you." (John 15:7)

Our acceptance with God, our access to Him, is all in Christ. As we consciously abide in Him we have the liberty to ask what we will, in the power of the new nature, and it shall be done. Let us keep this place and believe even now that our intercession is heard.

Specific Needs

____

____

____

____

DAY 30

What to Pray: For Worldwide Evangelism

Because our gospel comes to you not simply with words, but also with power, with the Holy Spirit and with deep conviction. (1 Thessalonians 1:5)
Those who have preached the gospel to you by the Holy Spirit sent from heaven. (1 Peter 1:12)

With modern technology the world seems to grow smaller every day. At the same time the world population is growing. Thus, more and more people need to hear the gospel, need to know Jesus Christ. Only as we and our missionaries labor in the power of the Spirit will we fulfill the task to "Go into all the world and preach the good news" (Mark 16:15).

How to Pray: Watching and Praying

Devote yourselves to prayer, being watchful and thankful. And pray for us, too, that God may open a door for our message, so that we may proclaim the mystery of Christ, for which I am in chains. (Colossians 4:2-3)

Do you not see how all depends upon God and prayer? As long as He lives and loves, hears and works, as long as there are people with hearts closed to the Word, we must pray without ceasing, devoting ourselves to prayer, that the door may be open to the gospel. These words are for every Christian.

Specific Needs

____

____

____

____

DAY 31

What to Pray: For the Spirit of Christ in His People

"I am the vine; you are the branches." (John 15:5)
"I have set you an example that you should do as I have done for you." (John 13:15)

As branches we are to be so like the Vine, so entirely identified with it, that all may see that we have the same nature, life and spirit. When we pray for the Spirit, let us not only think of the Spirit of power, but the very disposition and temperament of Jesus. Ask and expect nothing less for yourself and all God's people.

How to Pray: Striving in Prayer

Join me in my struggle by praying to God for me. (Romans 15:30)
I want you to know how much I am struggling for you . . . (Colossians 2:1)

The powers of evil seek to hinder us in prayer. Prayer is a conflict with opposing forces. It needs the whole heart and all our strength. May God give us grace to continue in prayer until we overcome.

Specific Needs